UNVEILI..G

MARSEILLE

Your Insider's Guide to the Multicultural Marvel

presented by

Discover your journey!

ll

Presented by Tailored Travel Guides
a WEST AGORA INT S.R.L. Brand
www.tailoredtravelguides.com

Edited by WEST AGORA INT S.R.L.
WEST AGORA INT S.R.L. All Rights Reserved
Copyright © WEST AGORA INT S.R.L., 2023

CONTENTS

MARSEILLE

FRANCE'S MULTICULTURAL MARVEL

Marseille, a historic port city on the Mediterranean coast, is France's second-largest city and one of its most vibrant and diverse destinations. Founded by Greek sailors over 2,600 years ago, the city has a rich history that is evident in its architecture, cultural heritage, and diverse population. Its stunning coastline, picturesque streets, and lively atmosphere make Marseille an irresistible destination for travelers seeking both adventure and relaxation.

From the bustling Vieux-Port to the ancient Le Panier district, Marseille is a city full of character and charm. Its colorful markets, world-class museums, and scenic landscapes make it a truly unique and inspiring place to visit. Whether you're interested in exploring the city's historic sites, sampling its delicious cuisine, or discovering hidden gems, this guide is designed to help you make the most of your stay in Marseille.

This in-depth travel guide provides all the information you need to plan a memorable trip to Marseille. With comprehensive details on top attractions, hidden gems, culinary delights, and more, we've got everything covered to ensure you have an unforgettable experience in this lively Mediterranean city. So, pack your bags, get ready to explore, and let's dive into the enchanting world of Marseille.

Bienvenue, dear traveler! Welcome to Marseille, the Mediterranean jewel where deep cultural heritage blends with a vibrant, cosmopolitan energy. As someone who has experienced the magic of Marseille firsthand, I'm delighted to help you uncover the hidden gems and experiences that only a true Marseillais would know.

Begin your Marseille adventure by embracing our customs, sharing warm "bonjour" greetings, and exchanging smiles and kind words with the people you meet as you traverse the city's bustling markets and sun-washed boulevards.

You may find yourself exploring the quaint streets of Le Panier, Marseille's oldest district. This neighborhood, with its narrow alleys and colorful buildings, is home to delightful local artisans, cozy cafes, and the beautiful Vieille Charité, a cultural center housed in a historic monument that speaks volumes of Marseille's rich history.

Take a detour off the beaten path and venture to the lesser-known but stunningly beautiful Parc Borely. This sprawling green space offers serene paths, botanical gardens, and a charming chateau-turned-museum that presents an incredible view of the Mediterranean Sea.

When hunger calls, seek out Chez Etienne, a local favorite tucked away in Le Panier. Known for its warm atmosphere and authentic cuisine, this restaurant serves traditional Marseillaise dishes, including the mouthwatering pizza fried in olive oil—a distinctive culinary experience that sets it apart from its Neapolitan counterpart.

As the sun starts its descent, consider a leisurely walk to Vallon des Auffes. This picturesque fishing port offers stunning views of the sea, traditional fishing huts, and quaint boats bobbing in the marina, setting the stage for an evening you'll remember.

In the heart of Marseille, pay a visit to Cours Julien when twilight descends. This vibrant square, known for its vivid murals and street art, comes alive with locals sharing stories over a pastis or indulging in boules, a traditional Provencal game. Join in, and let the eclectic spirit of the city draw you in.

As you explore Marseille, remember to savor each moment and let the city's distinctive charm envelop you. We, the locals, are always here to help, eager to share the magic of our captivating city with you. Bon voyage, dear traveler, and may your journey be filled with unforgettable memories!

PRACTICAL INFORMATION

Currency

The currency in Marseille, as in the rest of France, is the Euro (€). You can exchange your currency at banks, exchange offices, or ATMs. Credit cards are widely accepted, but it's a good idea to carry some cash for smaller purchases or businesses that don't accept cards.

Transportation

Marseille is well-connected by public transportation, including buses, trams, and the metro. The city's transportation system is operated by RTM (Régie des Transports Métropolitains). You can purchase single-ride tickets, 24-hour passes, or multi-day passes, depending on your needs. Taxis and ridesharing services like Uber are also available.

Driving in Marseille

If you plan on renting a car in Marseille, remember that driving in France is on the right side of the road. Ensure you have a valid driver's license and are aware of local traffic rules and regulations. Parking in the city center can be challenging, so consider using public transportation or park-and-ride facilities.

Language

French is the official language in Marseille, but many locals also speak English, especially in tourist areas. Learning a few basic phrases in French will help you communicate and show respect for the local culture.

Power sockets and adapters

France uses Type E power sockets with a voltage of 230V and a frequency of 50Hz. If your devices use a different plug type or voltage, you may need a power adapter or converter.

Shopping

Shops in Marseille are generally open from 9:00 am to 7:00 pm, Monday to Saturday. Some smaller shops may close for a lunch break. Supermarkets and larger stores may have extended hours and open on Sundays.

Tipping

Service charges are usually included in the bill at restaurants and cafes. However, it's customary to leave a small tip (5-10%) for good service. For taxi drivers, rounding up to the nearest Euro or adding 5-10% is appreciated.

USEFUL LINKS AND PHONE NUMBERS

Emergency Services

All Emergencies: 112
Police: 17
Fire Brigade: 18
Medical Emergencies (SAMU): 15

Transportation

Marseille Airport: +33 820 81 14 14, Marseille Airport
SNCF (French National Railway Company): +33 9 70 60 99 70, SNCF
RTM (Public Transport in Marseille): +33 4 91 91 92 10, RTM

Tourist Information

Marseille Tourism Office: +33 826 500 500, www.marseille-tourisme.com/en/
Tourist Map :
www.ontheworldmap.com/france/city/marseille/tourist-map-of-marseille-with-sightseeings.jpg

Hospitals

Assistance Publique – Hôpitaux de Marseille (AP-HM): +33 4 91 38 00 00, http://fr.ap-hm.fr/

City Government

City of Marseille: +33 4 91 55 11 11, www.marseille.fr

Maps

Marseille maps:
www.ontheworldmap.com/france/city/marseille/
Large detailed map of Marseille:
www.ontheworldmap.com/france/city/marseille/large-detailed-map-of-marseille.jpg
Map of Marseille City Center:
www.ontheworldmap.com/france/city/marseille/detailed-map-of-marseille-city-center.jpg
Marseille Metro map:
www.ontheworldmap.com/france/city/marseille/marseille-metro-map.jpg
Marseille Transport Map:
www.ontheworldmap.com/france/city/marseille/marseille-transport-map.jpg

Marseille

Ontheworldmap.com

TOP ATTRACTIONS IN MARSEILLE

VIEUX-PORT (OLD PORT)

Marseille's Vieux-Port is a bustling harbor and the heart of the city. Enjoy a stroll along the waterfront, take a boat trip to the nearby islands, or relax at one of the many cafes and restaurants offering stunning views of the port. Don't miss the daily fish market, where you can witness fishermen selling their fresh catch.

Website: https://t.ly/FeyB
Location: Quai des Belges, 13001 Marseille, France
Useful tips: The best time to visit the fish market is early in the morning. Make sure to wear comfortable shoes for walking.

BASILIQUE NOTRE-DAME DE LA GARDE

This iconic Catholic basilica sits atop a hill overlooking Marseille and offers panoramic views of the city, the harbor, and the Mediterranean Sea. Built in the 19th century, the basilica features a mix of Romanesque and Byzantine architectural styles and houses impressive mosaics and frescoes.

Website: http://www.notredamedelagarde.com/
Location: Rue Fort du Sanctuaire, 13281 Marseille, France
Useful tips: To reach the basilica, you can take the tourist train or bus 60 from the Vieux-Port. Keep in mind that there are steps to climb once you reach the site.

MUCEM (MUSEUM OF EUROPEAN AND MEDITERRANEAN CIVILISATIONS)

This modern museum, opened in 2013, is dedicated to European and Mediterranean civilizations, showcasing artifacts, art, and cultural exhibits. The striking building, designed by architect Rudy Ricciotti, features a latticework concrete shell that mimics the patterns of Mediterranean fishing nets.

Website: https://www.mucem.org/en
Location: 1 Esp. J4, 13002 Marseille, France
Useful tips: Plan at least 2-3 hours to explore the museum, and don't forget to visit the rooftop terrace for incredible views of the city and sea.

TOP ATTRACTIONS IN MARSEILLE

LE PANIER (OLD TOWN)

Le Panier is Marseille's historic district, with narrow streets, colorful houses, and a lively atmosphere. This charming neighborhood is perfect for exploring on foot, with art galleries, boutiques, and cafes waiting around every corner. Key sights include the Vieille Charité, a former almshouse turned cultural center, and the Maison Diamantée, a Renaissance-style mansion.

Website: https://t.ly/SAP-

Location: Le Panier, 13002 Marseille, France

Useful tips: Wear comfortable shoes for walking and explore at a leisurely pace to take in the area's charm and character.

CHÂTEAU D'IF

Located on a small island just off the coast of Marseille, the Château d'If is a 16th-century fortress that later became a notorious prison. Made famous by Alexandre Dumas' novel "The Count of Monte Cristo," the castle can be reached by a short boat trip from the Vieux-Port. Visitors can explore the fortress, the prison cells, and enjoy panoramic views of Marseille.

Website: https://t.ly/a_n5

Location: Île d'If, 13007 Marseille, France

Useful tips: Purchase tickets for the boat trip at the Vieux-Port, and make sure to bring sun protection and comfortable shoes.

LA CANEBIÈRE

This historic high street in the heart of Marseille offers a variety of shops, cafes, and restaurants, as well as beautiful architecture. The lively avenue is a perfect place to stroll, shop, or sit at a terrace to people-watch. From La Canebière, you can easily reach the Vieux-Port and other major attractions in the city.

Website: https://t.ly/t-IN

Location: La Canebière, 13001 Marseille, France

Useful tips: Explore side streets and small squares for hidden gems and local boutiques.

TOP ATTRACTIONS IN MARSEILLE

FORT SAINT-JEAN

Fort Saint-Jean is a historic fortress located at the entrance of Marseille's Old Port. With its origins dating back to the 17th century, the fort is an emblem of Marseille's rich history. Today, it is integrated into the MuCEM complex and offers stunning panoramic views over the city and the sea. A walk around the fort reveals well-preserved structures, beautiful gardens, and exceptional exhibitions.

Location: Prom. Robert Laffont, 13002 Marseille, France

Website: www.mucem.org/votre-visite/parcours-libres/du-j4-au-fort-saint-jean

Useful Tip: Make sure to explore the gardens within the fort and the footbridge that connects it to the MuCEM. Visiting at sunset provides a stunning backdrop for photographs.

LA VIEILLE CHARITÉ

La Vieille Charité is a magnificent Baroque building, originally built as an almshouse in the 17th century. Nestled in the heart of the Le Panier district, this architectural masterpiece now serves as a cultural center, housing several museums, including the Museum of Mediterranean Archaeology and the Museum of African, Oceanian, and Amerindian Arts. The internal courtyard, surrounded by pink and yellow stone arches, is a serene escape.

Location: 2 Rue de la Charité, 13002 Marseille, France

Website: https://vieille-charite-marseille.com/

Useful Tip: Check the cultural center's schedule before visiting as it frequently hosts temporary exhibitions, film screenings, and lectures. The charming café in the courtyard is a perfect spot for a break.

ABBAYE SAINT-VICTOR

One of the oldest places of Christian worship in Europe, the Abbaye Saint-Victor was founded in the 5th century. Named after the Roman soldier and Christian martyr, Saint Victor of Marseilles, this abbey is known for its striking Romanesque architecture and its crypt, which houses ancient sarcophagi. The abbey still functions as a church today and is a must-visit for history and architecture enthusiasts.

Location: Pl. Saint-Victor, 13007 Marseille, France

Website: www.saint-victor.net/?lang=fr

Useful Tip: Don't miss the crypt and the terraces, from which you can enjoy an outstanding view over the Old Port. Check the schedule for organ concerts and other religious ceremonies, which add to the atmosphere of this historical site.

TOP ATTRACTIONS IN MARSEILLE

PALAIS DU PHARO

Perched on a cliff overlooking the Old Port, the Palais du Pharo is an imposing palace originally built for Napoleon III. Today, this grand structure functions as a conference center but is also open for visitors to explore. The palace is surrounded by a spacious park that offers one of the most stunning panoramic views of Marseille, making it a perfect spot for picnics and leisurely strolls.

Location: 58 Bd Charles Livon, 13007 Marseille, France

Website: https://palaisdupharo.marseille.fr/

Useful Tip: Take a walk in the surrounding gardens, where you can enjoy a relaxing break with a view. The gardens are free to enter, and the view of the Old Port is breathtaking, especially at sunset.

MUSÉE DES BEAUX-ARTS (MUSEUM OF FINE ARTS)

Housed in a grand 19th-century palace, the Museum of Fine Arts in Marseille is one of France's oldest art museums. It hosts an impressive collection of European paintings from the 16th to 19th centuries, including works by Rubens, Courbet, and Delacroix, as well as sculptures and modern art. The museum's elegant and spacious galleries offer a serene and enriching experience for art lovers.

Location: Palais Longchamp Aile gauche, 9 Rue Edouard Stephan, 13004 Marseille, France

Website: https://musees.marseille.fr/musee-des-beaux-arts-mba

Useful Tip: After visiting the museum, explore the surrounding Palais Longchamp and its beautiful gardens. There are often temporary exhibitions at the museum, so check the website for the latest information.

SAINT LAURENT CHURCH

The Saint Laurent Church is a historic Romanesque church that stands as a sentinel over the Old Port of Marseille. This beautiful stone church, constructed in the 12th century, is one of the oldest in Marseille. Its interior is serene and austere, offering a peaceful respite from the bustling city. The church is located on a hill, providing stunning views of the city and the sea.

Location: 16 Esp. de la Tourette, 13002 Marseille, France

Website: https://notredamedelamajor.fr/

Useful Tip: Take the time to climb the hill to the church, as it offers some of the best views over the Old Port. The church is still active, so be respectful of services if you visit.

HIDDEN GEMS AND LESSER-KNOWN SIGHTS IN MARSEILLE

LE VALLON DES AUFFES

This picturesque fishing village is a serene gem nestled along the rocky coastline of Marseille. With its traditional fishing huts, small boats bobbing in the azure water, and narrow, winding streets, Le Vallon des Auffes feels like a step back in time. Despite being close to the city center, it retains an authentic and peaceful ambiance, offering a unique glimpse into Marseille's maritime heritage. Dining here is a treat; the waterfront is dotted with small, intimate restaurants where the seafood is as fresh as it gets. The renowned Chez Fonfon is a particular highlight, known for its bouillabaisse, a traditional Provençal fish stew that is a must-try in Marseille. A stroll along the stone pathways reveals charming houses adorned with colorful shutters and locals going about their daily routines, providing visitors with a relaxed and deeply local experience of life in Marseille.

Website: www.marseilletourisme.fr/fr/que-voir/patrimoine-culture/quartiers/vallon-auffes/
Location: Vallon des Auffes, 13007 Marseille, France
Useful tips: Visit during sunset for a magical atmosphere and stunning views. If you plan to dine at Chez Fonfon or any of the other popular restaurants, make a reservation in advance to secure a table by the water.

LA FRICHE BELLE DE MAI

A former tobacco factory, La Friche Belle de Mai is now a thriving cultural center, with art galleries, performance spaces, a skate park, and more. The space hosts numerous events throughout the year, including concerts, exhibitions, and film screenings. The rooftop terrace offers panoramic views of the city and is a popular spot for drinks and events during the summer months.

Website: www.lafriche.org
Location: 41 Rue Jobin, 13003 Marseille, France
Useful tips: Check their event calendar before visiting to make the most of your trip.

LE COURS JULIEN

Le Cours Julien is a lively, bohemian district in Marseille that offers a taste of the city's creative and alternative scene. Explore its pedestrian streets lined with trendy bars, restaurants, and boutiques, and discover numerous murals and street art that give the area its vibrant and artistic character. This neighborhood also hosts various markets, music events, and outdoor performances, making it a cultural hotspot. Here, visitors can also find unique bookshops, artisan craft stores, and art galleries, further contributing to the district's reputation as a hub for creatives and lovers of unique finds.

Website: https://www.marseille-tourisme.com/decouvrez-marseille/culture-et-patrimoine/les-111-quartiers-marseillais/le-cours-julien/

Location: Cours Julien, 13006 Marseille, France

Useful tips: Visit on a Wednesday or Saturday morning to experience the popular organic market.

MARSEILLE'S SOAP FACTORIES

Marseille is famous for its traditional soap, known as Savon de Marseille. A few remaining factories in the city still produce this soap in the traditional way, offering a glimpse into a craft that has been part of Marseille's heritage for centuries. The soap is made primarily with olive oil and is known for its pure and natural ingredients. A visit to one of these factories is a unique and aromatic journey into Marseille's past.

Location:

Le Fer à Cheval 66 Chemin de Sainte Marthe 13014 Marseille – (Shop and factory) 04 91 10 30 80; Le Serail 50, Bd Anatole de la Forge 13014 Marseille (Shop and factory) 04 91 98 28 25; Savonnerie du Midi 72, Rue Augustin Roux 13015 Marseille (Museum, shop and factory) 04 91 60 54 04; La Savonnerie Marius Fabre 148 Avenue Paul Bourret, 13300 Salon-de-Provence 04 90 53 24 77

Website: www.marseille-tourisme.com/en/discover-marseille/traditions/marseille-soap/

Useful Tip: Take advantage of your visit to buy authentic Savon de Marseille directly from the factory as a unique souvenir or gift. Check the website for guided tour availability.

HIDDEN GEMS AND LESSER-KNOWN SIGHTS IN MARSEILLE

LE JARDIN DES VESTIGES

The Jardin des Vestiges is a surprising archaeological site in the heart of Marseille. It reveals the ancient Greek port from which the city originated more than 2,600 years ago. The garden is a peaceful oasis amid the urban hustle and provides a tangible connection to the city's ancient history, with remnants of city walls, port facilities, and public buildings. As you wander through the serene paths, you will find informative plaques detailing the history of each ruin, transporting you back to a time when Marseille was a bustling Greek port city. It's a tranquil, reflective space where the city's vibrant present meets its rich past..

Location: 2 Rue Henri Barbusse, 13001 Marseille, France

Website: www.marseilletourisme.fr/fr/que-voir/patrimoine-culture/parcs-jardins/jardin-vestiges/

Useful Tip: The garden is located beside the Marseille History Museum, so consider pairing the two for a deep dive into the city's past. Be sure to bring a camera to capture the unique juxtaposition of ancient ruins set against modern Marseille.

LA CARAVELLE

La Caravelle is a historic bar nestled on the second floor of the Hôtel Belle-Vue, offering spectacular views of the Old Port from its charming balcony. This bar retains a vintage 1950s style and is a beloved secret spot for locals. With its Jazz tunes, excellent cocktails, and maritime-inspired decor, it offers a unique and intimate experience in Marseille.

Location: 34 Quai du Port, 13002 Marseille, France

Website: http://www.lacaravelle-marseille.com/

Useful Tip: Arrive early, especially in the evening, as the balcony seats with the best views fill up quickly. Check the website for live music events.

PARKS AND GARDENS IN MARSEILLE

PARC BORÉLY

Parc Borély is a popular 17-hectare park located near the beach. It boasts beautiful French gardens, English gardens, and a rose garden. Visitors can enjoy activities such as rowing on the lake, cycling, and picnicking. The park is also home to the Museum of Decorative Arts, Fashion and Ceramics.

Website: https://t.ly/ROye
Location: Avenue du Prado, 13008 Marseille, France
Useful tips: There are many restaurants and cafes nearby, making it a great spot for a full day out.

PARC DE LA MAISON BLANCHE

This beautiful park is a true oasis within the city. Parc de la Maison Blanche features a diverse range of flora and fauna, making it a perfect destination for nature lovers. There are walking paths, playgrounds, and picnic areas, making it an ideal spot for a relaxing day out.

Website: https://t.ly/lJms
Location: 16 Boulevard de la Viste, 13015 Marseille, France
Useful tips: There is an onsite restaurant and ample parking available.

LE JARDIN DU PHARO

Le Jardin du Pharo is a beautiful public garden surrounding the Palais du Pharo, which offers stunning views of the Old Port and the city. The garden is well-maintained and provides a peaceful escape from the bustling city. It is an ideal spot for picnics, leisurely strolls, or simply admiring the view.

Website: https://t.ly/m1FO
Location: 58 Boulevard Charles Livon, 13007 Marseille, France
Useful tips: Take a walk along the nearby Corniche Kennedy for more breathtaking views of the Mediterranean Sea.

PARKS AND GARDENS IN MARSEILLE

JARDIN DE LA MAGALONE

Jardin de la Magalone is a hidden gem in the city, featuring an 18th-century bastide and a beautifully designed park with traditional French and Italianate gardens. It is a perfect destination for a peaceful walk or a quiet picnic, as you take in the surrounding sculptures, fountains, and greenery.

Website: https://t.ly/k-Rj

Location: 245 Boulevard Michelet, 13009 Marseille, France

Useful tips: Entrance is free, but opening hours vary depending on the season. Make sure to check the official website for the latest information.

PARC LONGCHAMP

Parc Longchamp is one of Marseille's grandest and most iconic green spaces. Located behind the monumental Palais Longchamp, this park is a great place for both relaxation and recreation. It features vast lawns, beautiful fountains, a botanical garden, and a small zoo. The park's striking architecture and abundant shade trees make it a popular gathering spot for locals and visitors alike. It's a serene oasis offering a breath of fresh air in the urban environment of Marseille.

Location: Boulevard Jardin Zoologique, 13004 Marseille, France

Website: www.marseilletourisme.fr/en/places-see/heritage-culture/parks-gardens/parc-longchamps/

Useful Tip: Don't miss the Museum of Natural History and the Museum of Fine Arts, both located within the Palais Longchamp, which overlooks the park. The park is also a popular spot for picnics, so consider bringing some local treats to enjoy.

PARC DU 26ÈME CENTENAIRE

The Parc du 26ème Centenaire is a spacious and modern park located in the heart of Marseille. Named in commemoration of Marseille's 2,600th anniversary, this park is known for its beautiful landscaped gardens, large pond with fountains, and several themed gardens, including a Japanese garden and a Mediterranean garden. It is a favorite for families, with dedicated play areas for children and plenty of space for picnics and outdoor activities.

Location: Place Zino Francescatti, 13010 Marseille, France

Website: www.marseille.fr/environnement/presentation

Useful Tip: This park is quite expansive, so be sure to wear comfortable walking shoes. There is a small train that provides tours of the park - a great option for those with limited mobility or for families with young children.

MARSEILLE'S CULINARY SCENE

L'ÉPUISETTE

Perched on the edge of the sea, L'Épuisette offers a Michelin-starred dining experience with breathtaking views of the Mediterranean. Its menu showcases the freshest seafood, including the iconic bouillabaisse.
Address: 158 Rue du Vallon des Auffes, 13007 Marseille, France
Website: www.l-epuisette.fr
Tip: Request a table on the terrace for a dining experience with an exceptional sea view.

CHEZ FONFON

A family-run establishment since 1952, Chez Fonfon is renowned for its authentic bouillabaisse. The atmosphere is warm and inviting, making it a quintessential Marseillais experience.
Address: 140 Rue du Vallon des Auffes, 13007 Marseille, France
Website: www.chez-fonfon.com
Tip: Make sure to save room for their traditional tarte tropézienne dessert.

LE FOUR DES NAVETTES

The oldest bakery in the city, Le Four des Navettes has been delighting locals and visitors since 1781 with its famous boat-shaped cookies flavored with orange blossom.
Address: 136 Rue Sainte, 13007 Marseille, France
Website: www.fourdesnavettes.com
Tip: Pair a navette with a cup of fresh Provençal lavender tea for a true local experience.

BAR DE LA MARINE

A classic and historic bar in the Old Port of Marseille, Bar de la Marine is the perfect spot for a casual drink. Here you can enjoy a glass of pastis, the city's signature aperitif, while soaking in the vibrant port atmosphere.
Address: 15 Quai de Rive Neuve, 13007 Marseille, France
Website: www.facebook.com/bardelamarineofficiel
Tip: Arrive early in the evening to secure a table on the terrace and enjoy the sunset over the Old Port.

MARSEILLE'S CULINARY SCENE

BOUILLABAISSE

Marseille is famous for its traditional fish stew, Bouillabaisse, which is a must-try when visiting the city. Made from a variety of fish, shellfish, and other seafood, Bouillabaisse is typically served with rouille, a garlicky mayonnaise, and crusty bread.

Tip: Enhance your Bouillabaisse experience by pairing it with a crisp and aromatic Provencal white wine, which complements the rich flavors of the stew beautifully.

NAVETTES

Navettes are traditional boat-shaped cookies from Marseille that are flavored with orange blossom water. They are typically enjoyed with coffee or tea and can be found at various bakeries throughout the city.

Tip: Try dipping a Navette in a cup of strong black coffee or a floral herbal tea; the slight bitterness or delicate aroma perfectly balances the sweet and fragrant flavors of this traditional treat.

PIZZAS AND PANISSES

Marseille has a strong influence from Italian cuisine due to its proximity to Italy and its history of Italian immigrants. As a result, you can find some amazing pizza places in the city.

Tip: Pair your pizza with a local Provencal rosé wine or a chilled glass of pastis, an anise-flavored aperitif beloved in Marseille, to truly savor the blend of Italian influence and local tradition.

PASTIS

When in Marseille, be sure to taste Pastis, an anise-flavored aperitif that is synonymous with the city. You can find Pastis in almost every café and bar, served with a side of water to dilute the strong flavor.

Tip: Try pairing Pastis with traditional Provençal olives or tapenade on crusty bread as a delightful accompaniment that complements the herbal notes of this iconic Marseille drink.

SHOPPING IN MARSEILLE

LE PANIER

Le Panier is the oldest neighborhood in Marseille, filled with narrow streets, colorful buildings, and a variety of local shops. This area is perfect for finding unique souvenirs, handmade crafts, and regional products. Wander the picturesque streets and explore the many boutiques, art galleries, and artisan workshops.

Website: N/A

Location: Le Panier, 13002 Marseille, France

Useful tips: While shopping, take time to appreciate the street art and murals that adorn the walls of Le Panier.

LES TERRASSES DU PORT

Les Terrasses du Port is a modern shopping center with a wide range of international and local brands. Located near the port, it offers a beautiful view of the Mediterranean Sea from its terrace. Enjoy a shopping spree followed by a meal at one of the numerous restaurants available on-site.

Website: www.lesterrassesduport.com

Location: 9 Quai du Lazaret, 13002 Marseille, France

Useful tips: Take a break on the terrace to appreciate the views of the sea and the city skyline.

RUE SAINT-FERRÉOL

Rue Saint-Ferréol is a pedestrian street in the heart of Marseille and a popular shopping destination. Lined with clothing stores, boutiques, and cafés, this bustling street offers a mix of high-street brands and local shops. Don't miss the nearby Centre Bourse, a large shopping center with a diverse range of retailers.

Location: Rue Saint-Ferréol, 13001 Marseille, France

Useful tips: Keep an eye out for sales and promotions to make the most of your shopping experience.

SHOPPING IN MARSEILLE

NOAILLES MARKET

Noailles Market is a vibrant, bustling market in the center of Marseille. Known as the "belly of Marseille," it offers a unique shopping experience, featuring a variety of stalls selling fresh produce, spices, and delicacies from around the world. Get lost in the vibrant colors and fragrances of this multicultural market.

Location: Noailles, 13001 Marseille, France

Useful tips: Go early in the day to enjoy the liveliest atmosphere and best selection of goods. Don't forget to try some of the delicious street food available.

LA MAISON EMPEREUR

La Maison Empereur, established in 1827, is the oldest hardware store in France and a must-visit for anyone who appreciates traditional craftsmanship. This family-owned store offers a variety of goods, from kitchenware to gardening tools, as well as Marseille's famous soap. The store's atmosphere and carefully curated collection make it a unique shopping destination.

Website: www.empereur.fr/en/

Location: 4 Rue des Récolettes, 13001 Marseille, France

Useful tips: Take your time to explore the store and find unique and authentic souvenirs to bring back home.

LA CANEBIÈRE

La Canebière is a historic boulevard in Marseille that stretches from the Old Port to the Reformés neighborhood. It is a vibrant area filled with shops, restaurants, and cafés, making it an excellent destination for shopping and dining. Discover a mix of high-street retailers and local businesses while strolling along this iconic street.

Location: La Canebière, 13001 Marseille, France

Useful tips: Don't miss the monthly market held on La Canebière, offering regional products, crafts, and street performances.

FAMILY-FRIENDLY ACTIVITIES IN MARSEILLE

OK CORRAL THEME PARK

OK Corral is a Wild West-themed amusement park, offering a fun-filled day for the entire family. With a range of attractions including roller coasters, water slides, and shows, there's something for everyone to enjoy. The park also has a petting zoo and pony rides for younger kids.

Website: www.okcorral.fr
Location: 13780 Cuges-les-Pins, France (about 40 km from Marseille)
Useful tips: Check the website for opening hours and special offers.

CITY AVENTURE MARSEILLE

For an active day out, head to City Aventure Marseille, an outdoor adventure park set in the lush hills of La Colline. The park offers treetop climbing courses for all ages and skill levels, including courses designed for young children. The park also has a playground, picnic area, and a zip line.
Website: www.cityaventure.com/en/
Location: 225 Chemin des Trois Pères, 13012 Marseille, France
Useful tips: Wear comfortable clothing and closed-toe shoes.

LE PETIT TRAIN DE MARSEILLE

Le Petit Train de Marseille is a charming way to explore the city with kids. The small train takes visitors on a guided tour through the historic districts, providing an informative and fun experience. Choose between two routes: one exploring the Old Port and Panier district, and the other climbing to Notre-Dame de la Garde.
Website: http://www.petit-train-marseille.com/
Location: 86 Quai du Port, 13002 Marseille, France
Useful tips: Buy tickets online in advance to secure your spot and save time.

PARC LONGCHAMP

Parc Longchamp is a perfect spot for a family outing. With its vast green spaces, impressive fountains, and playgrounds, there's plenty of room for kids to roam and play. The park also houses the Museum of Natural History and the Museum of Fine Arts, where you can introduce your children to the world of art and science. The park is also house to a zoo.
Website: https://t.ly/F1RQ
Location: Boulevard Jardin Zoologique, 13004 Marseille, France
Useful tips: Entrance to the park is free, but there are admission fees for the museums and zoo.

FAMILY-FRIENDLY ACTIVITIES IN MARSEILLE

PARC MARIN DE LA CÔTE BLEUE

Embark on an exciting eco-tourism adventure at the Parc Marin de la Côte Bleue, a marine park located west of Marseille. Its rich biodiversity, including numerous species of fish and the gorgeous Posidonia seagrass meadows, will captivate marine life enthusiasts. The park is also involved in various conservation efforts, providing an educational experience for all ages. Boat tours are offered for those wishing to explore the marine park's wonders.

Website: www.parcmarincotebleue.fr

Location: Carry-le-Rouet, 13620, France (Headquarters of the park)

Useful tips: Book your boat tour ahead of time, especially during the summer months when demand is high.

THE FRIOUL ARCHIPELAGO

A short boat ride from Marseille takes you to the Frioul Archipelago, an excellent destination for a family day trip. The islands of Ratonneau and Pomègues offer beautiful landscapes, beaches, and walking trails. You can also visit the historic Château d'If, which inspired Alexandre Dumas' novel "The Count of Monte Cristo."

Website: http://www.frioul-if-express.com/

Location: Boat departure from Quai des Belges, 13001 Marseille, France

Useful tips: Bring sunscreen and a hat, as shade is limited on the islands.

MUCEM - MUSEUM OF EUROPEAN AND MEDITERRANEAN CIVILISATIONS

The Mucem is an iconic cultural institution in Marseille, offering a unique perspective on Mediterranean history and culture. Its exhibits cover various topics, from art and religion to migration and the environment. The museum's impressive architecture and stunning sea views make it an ideal destination for families.

Website: https://www.mucem.org/

Location: 7 Prom. Robert Laffont, 13002 Marseille, France

Useful tips: Children under 18 enter for free. Don't miss the suspended footbridge connecting the museum to Fort Saint-Nicolas.

MARSEILLE BY NIGHT

ILLUMINATED MONUMENTS AND EVENING STROLLS

OLD PORT (VIEUX-PORT)

The Old Port is the heart and soul of Marseille and is a hive of activity day and night. As the evening sets in, the port becomes a beautifully lit spectacle, making it an ideal spot for a relaxed evening stroll. The numerous bars and restaurants around the port also come alive with locals and tourists alike.
Location: Quai des Belges, 13002 Marseille, France
Tip: Enjoy the lively atmosphere but beware of pickpockets in crowded areas.

NOTRE-DAME DE LA GARDE

The iconic Notre-Dame de la Garde, perched high above the city, is beautifully lit up at night, serving as a beacon overlooking Marseille. The panoramic view of the city's night lights from the basilica is nothing short of breathtaking.
Location: Rue Fort du Sanctuaire, 13281 Marseille, France
Tip: The hill can be quite a climb, consider taking the tourist train or a taxi.

LA CANEBIÈRE

La Canebière, the historic high street in the old quarter of Marseille, is a vibrant area day and night. The buildings along this famous stretch are beautifully lit, providing a wonderful backdrop for a nighttime walk.
Location: La Canebière, 13001 Marseille, France
Tip: Explore the side streets off La Canebière for unique shops and cafes.

MARSEILLE BY NIGHT

BARS AND PUBS

LA CARAVELLE

Tucked away on the old port's side, La Caravelle is an institution in Marseille. It offers a panoramic view over the port while you enjoy your cocktail, local wine, or beer. The bar hosts regular jazz nights, adding an extra layer of charm.

Location: 34 Quai du Port, 13002 Marseille, France

Tip: Try to grab a window seat for the best views. Also, the bar can get busy, so be prepared for a wait.

Website: http://www.lacaravelle-marseille.com/

LE BAR DE LA MARINE

Featured in Marcel Pagnol's movies, this historic bar on the old port has a distinctive nostalgic ambiance. Sip on your pastis or beer while soaking up the vintage atmosphere.

Location: 15 Quai de Rive Neuve, 13007 Marseille, France

Tip: The terrace seating is perfect for people watching.

Website: https://www.facebook.com/bardelamarineofficiel

LA RHUMERIE

Offering a wide selection of rum-based drinks, La Rhumerie is a cozy spot to end your day. The bar's Caribbean theme makes for a unique atmosphere.

Location: 19 Rue Fort Notre Dame, 13007 Marseille, France

Tip: If you're new to rum, ask the knowledgeable staff for recommendations.

Website: www.larhumerie-marseille.com

MARSEILLE BY NIGHT

NIGHTCLUBS AND DANCE CLUBS

LE BABY

Le Baby is a popular nightclub in Marseille known for its electric atmosphere and great DJs spinning a variety of music from techno to hip-hop.
Location: 2 Rue André Poggioli, 13006 Marseille, France
Tip: Be prepared for late nights as the party doesn't get started until well past midnight.
Website: www.facebook.com/babyclubmarseille/

SPARTACUS CLUB

Located a bit outside of Marseille, Spartacus Club is one of the biggest clubs in the region. It's known for its high-energy electronic music and hosts internationally renowned DJs.
Location: 141 Route de la Télévision, 13190 Allauch, France
Tip: This club is a bit off the beaten path, so it's best to plan your transport ahead. It's worth the trip if you're an electronic music fan.
Website: www.facebook.com/thebeezspartacus/

L'INTERMÉDIAIRE LIVE

L'Intermédiaire Live is a lively and intimate nightclub that showcases a diverse range of music, from live bands playing jazz and funk to DJs setting the dance floor alight with electronic beats. It's a place where locals and visitors mingle freely in a convivial atmosphere.
Location: 63 Place Jean Jaurès, 13006 Marseille, France
Tip: Check their schedule in advance, as they often host themed nights and live performances that you won't want to miss.
Website: www.facebook.com/Intermediaire.live

MARSEILLE BY NIGHT

LATE-NIGHT DINING

LA CARAVELLE

Situated in the Vieux-Port area, La Caravelle is a charming restaurant offering a variety of French dishes. It's the perfect spot to enjoy a late-night meal with views of the harbor.

Location: 34 Quai du Port, 13002 Marseille, France

Tip: Try their tapas and cocktails. Reservations are recommended due to its popularity.

Website: http://www.lacaravelle-marseille.com/

L'AROMAT

If you're looking to taste some authentic local cuisine, L'Aromat is the place to be. They serve delectable Provençal dishes until late.

Location: 49 Rue Sainte, 13001 Marseille, France

Tip: Be sure to try their version of the traditional bouillabaisse.

Website: www.laromat.com

LE P'TIT TROQUET

This cozy bistro offers a delightful range of traditional French dishes. Open until midnight, it's ideal for a late-night dining experience.

Location: 72 Quai du Port, 13002 Marseille, France

Tip: Check out their impressive selection of regional wines.

Website: www.restaurant-le-ptit-jardin-marseille.fr

MARSEILLE BY NIGHT

NIGHTLIFE AREAS

LE COURS JULIEN

Le Cours Julien is the city's cultural hub, hosting an eclectic mix of bars, live music venues, and independent shops. Street art covers the walls, giving this area a unique atmosphere that comes alive at night.
Location: Cours Julien, 13006 Marseille, France
Tip: Be sure to visit La Dame Noir, a local favorite bar for its atmosphere and music.

LE VIEUX-PORT

The Old Port is a bustling place both day and night, filled with bars, restaurants, and nightclubs. The ambiance is electric, making it a popular nightlife spot among locals and tourists alike.
Location: Le Vieux Port, 13002 Marseille, France
Tip: Try to catch a sunset here before your night begins; the view is stunning.

LA PLAINE

La Plaine, also known as Place Jean-Jaurès, is a vibrant district with a young, bohemian vibe. It's packed with hip bars, clubs, and eateries that stay open until late.
Location: Place Jean-Jaurès, 13005 Marseille, France
Tip: Check out Café Julien, a popular venue for concerts and DJs.

SAFETY TIPS

- Be aware of your surroundings and keep an eye on your belongings, as pickpocketing can be an issue in crowded areas.
- Stick to well-lit streets and avoid wandering into unfamiliar, poorly lit areas late at night.
- Use reputable taxi services or ride-sharing apps to get around at night, especially if you are unfamiliar with the area. **Tip:** Save the phone number of a trusted taxi company in your phone for convenience.
- When enjoying the vibrant nightlife, always keep your drink in sight and never accept drinks from strangers. **Tip:** Drinking responsibly and staying hydrated will help ensure a safer and more enjoyable night out.
- Keep emergency contact numbers handy, including local police and your country's embassy.
- Carry a photocopy of your passport and other important documents, leaving the originals in a safe place.

By following these tips and exploring the city by night, you'll be able to experience the magic and charm of the city while staying safe and having an unforgettable time.

ART AND CULTURE IN MARSEILLE

MUCEM (MUSEUM OF EUROPEAN AND MEDITERRANEAN CIVILIZATIONS)

The MuCEM is a stunning architectural masterpiece dedicated to the cultures and histories of the Mediterranean region. This museum not only hosts exhibitions, film screenings, and live performances that celebrate the rich history of the area, but also serves as a research center and a space for public debates and seminars. Don't miss the striking Rudy Ricciotti-designed building, a masterpiece of concrete lacework, and its seamless blend with the 17th-century Fort Saint-Jean, which is also part of the museum complex.

Website: www.mucem.org

Location: 1 Esp. J4, 13002 Marseille, France

Useful tips: Visit the rooftop terrace for breathtaking views of the city and the sea. Consider visiting in late afternoon to enjoy the sunset from this remarkable vantage point.

LA FRICHE LA BELLE DE MAI

Once an old tobacco factory, La Friche la Belle de Mai has been transformed into a thriving cultural center. This multifaceted space houses art galleries, theaters, music venues, workshops, and more. It's a melting pot of creativity, providing a space for artistic experimentation and collaboration.

Website: www.lafriche.org

Location: 41 Rue Jobin, 13003 Marseille, France

Useful tips: Check the events calendar on their website for special events and performances.

LE PANIER DISTRICT

Le Panier is the oldest district in Marseille and a charming maze of narrow, cobbled streets. Rich in history and culture, the area is home to several museums, galleries, and art studios, including the Maison Diamantée and the Musée des Docks Romains. Stroll around Le Panier to discover colorful street art, boutiques, and cozy cafés.

Location: Le Panier, 13002 Marseille, France

Useful tips: Take a walking tour to learn more about the history and hidden gems of this fascinating district.

VIEILLE CHARITÉ

Vieille Charité is a former almshouse and a striking architectural gem located in the heart of Le Panier district. This beautifully restored 17th-century complex now houses cultural institutions, including the Mediterranean Archeology Museum and the Museum of African, Oceanic, and Amerindian Arts. It also hosts temporary exhibitions and events throughout the year.

Website: http://vieille-charite-marseille.com/

Location: 2 Rue de la Charité, 13002 Marseille, France

Useful tips: Take a break at the café located in the central courtyard and soak in the stunning architecture.

THE CANTINI MUSEUM

The Cantini Museum is dedicated to modern art from the early 20th century to the 1960s. The museum's collection boasts works by renowned artists such as Picasso, Léger, and Kandinsky. Housed in a magnificent 17th-century building, the Cantini Museum offers visitors a chance to explore the evolution of modern art in an elegant setting.

Website: www.musees.marseille.fr/musee-cantini-0

Location: 19 Rue Grignan, 13006 Marseille, France

Useful tips: Enjoy the impressive collection of art nouveau glassware on display.

ART AND CULTURE IN MARSEILLE

THE MUSEUM OF FINE ARTS

Located within the stunning Palais Longchamp, the Museum of Fine Arts in Marseille houses a remarkable collection of European paintings and sculptures from the 16th to the 19th centuries. The museum features works by renowned artists such as Rubens, Courbet, and Ingres. This institution is one of the oldest museums in the city, and its neoclassical architecture alone is worth a visit. The museum frequently hosts temporary exhibitions and cultural events that complement its permanent collection, making it a dynamic and ever-evolving space for art lovers.

Website: www.musees.marseille.fr/musee-des-beaux-arts-mba
Location: Palais Longchamp, Rue Espérandieu, 13004 Marseille, France
Useful tips: After exploring the museum, take a leisurely walk in the picturesque Parc Longchamp. It is also advisable to check the museum's schedule for guided tours and special exhibitions.

THE MUSEUM OF MEDITERRANEAN ARCHAEOLOGY

Housed in the historic La Vieille Charité complex in the heart of the Panier district, the Museum of Mediterranean Archaeology boasts one of France's most extensive collections of ancient artifacts. The museum showcases a wide range of pieces from the Mediterranean basin, including Egyptian mummies, Greek ceramics, and Middle Eastern antiquities. The exhibits are thoughtfully arranged and trace the rich, interconnected histories of the region's ancient civilizations. The museum aims to be more than just a repository of artifacts; it is a center for learning and engagement with the ancient world.

Website: https://musees.marseille.fr/musee-darcheologie-mediterraneenne-mam
Location: 2 Rue de la Charité, 13002 Marseille, France
Useful tips: The museum is part of the La Vieille Charité complex, which also includes several other cultural institutions; plan to spend a few hours exploring the entire site. Keep an eye out for the museum's regular temporary exhibitions, which dive deeper into specific aspects of Mediterranean history.

HISTORICAL AND ARCHITECTURAL LANDMARKS IN MARSEILLE

BASILIQUE NOTRE-DAME DE LA GARDE

Perched atop the highest point in Marseille, the Basilique Notre-Dame de la Garde is a symbol of the city and a must-visit. This Neo-Byzantine basilica offers stunning panoramic views of Marseille, the Old Port, and the Mediterranean Sea. Inside, admire the beautiful mosaics and maritime-themed ex-votos.

Website: https://www.notredamedelagarde.fr/

Location: Rue Fort du Sanctuaire, 13281 Marseille, France

Useful tips: The walk up to the basilica is steep, so consider taking the tourist train or city bus.

LE PANIER

Le Panier is Marseille's oldest district, known for its narrow winding streets, colorful houses, and artistic atmosphere. Wander the area's charming alleys, visit galleries and boutiques, or stop at a café to soak up the ambiance. Don't miss the striking modernist architecture of La Vieille Charité, a former almshouse now housing museums and cultural centers.

Location: Le Panier, 13002 Marseille, France

Useful tips: Wear comfortable walking shoes and explore at a leisurely pace.

PALAIS LONGCHAMP

The Palais Longchamp is a stunning architectural masterpiece built in the 19th century to celebrate the arrival of water from the Durance River. The palace is home to the Museum of Fine Arts and the Museum of Natural History. Its impressive colonnade, fountains, and statues are set in the beautiful Parc Longchamp.

Website: https://t.ly/gG2X

Location: Boulevard Jardin Zoologique, 13004 Marseille, France

Useful tips: Combine your visit to the palace with a stroll through Parc Longchamp.

HISTORICAL AND ARCHITECTURAL LANDMARKS IN MARSEILLE

LA MAJOR CATHEDRAL

La Major Cathedral, also known as Cathédrale Sainte-Marie-Majeure, is a striking Roman-Byzantine style structure overlooking the Old Port. Built between 1852 and 1893, it features an impressive façade adorned with domes, turrets, and colorful stone stripes. The vast interior is equally impressive, boasting stunning mosaics and stained-glass windows.

Website: www.marseille-tourisme.com/en/discover-marseille/culture-heritage/discover-the-sites-and-monuments-in-marseille/cathedrale-de-la-major-marseilles-cathedral/

Location: Place de la Major, 13002 Marseille, France

Useful tips: Free entry; the cathedral is open daily except during services.

FORT SAINT-NICOLAS

Fort Saint-Nicolas, built in the 17th century by Louis XIV, is a historic fortification overlooking the Old Port. Initially designed to defend the city from naval attacks, the fort later served as a prison and military barracks. Enjoy spectacular views of the harbor and the nearby Fort Saint-Jean from its ramparts.

Website: www.lacitadelledemarseille.org

Location: Mnt du Souvenir Français, 13007 Marseille, France

Useful tips: The fort itself is only open during special events, but the surrounding park offers lovely views and is open year-round.

CHÂTEAU D'IF

Located on a small island in the Bay of Marseille, Château d'If is a 16th-century fortress that gained fame as the setting for Alexandre Dumas' novel "The Count of Monte Cristo." Once a notorious prison, the castle is now a popular tourist destination. Visitors can explore the fortress, enjoy stunning views of Marseille, and learn about the history of the island.

Website: http://www.chateau-if.fr/en/

Location: Embarcadère Frioul If, 1 Quai de la Fraternité, 13001 Marseille, France

Useful tips: A 20-minute boat ride is required to reach the island; boats depart from the Old Port.

HÔTEL DE VILLE

The Hôtel de Ville, or City Hall, of Marseille is a striking example of French Baroque architecture and serves as one of the city's prominent landmarks. Constructed in the 17th century, this ornate building is situated in the historic district of Le Panier and stands as a symbol of Marseille's civic pride. It is adorned with beautiful sculptures and overlooks the bustling Old Port of Marseille. The square in front of the Hôtel de Ville, known as the Place de l'Hôtel de Ville, is a lively spot where locals and tourists alike enjoy the vibrant atmosphere of Marseille.

Website: http://www.marseille.fr/

Location: Pl. Villeneuve-Bargemon, 13002 Marseille, France

Useful tips: The building itself is not generally open to the public as it is a working government building, but the exterior is worth admiring. The surrounding area is filled with charming cafes and shops, perfect for leisurely exploration after viewing the Hôtel de Ville.

MAISON DIAMANTÉE

The Maison Diamantée, or "Diamond House," is a striking 16th-century Renaissance building adorned with a unique diamond-point façade. This architectural gem once served as the residence of Marseille's aristocrats and now houses the Musee du Vieux Marseille, which explores the history and traditions of the city.

Location: 3 Rue de la Prison, 13002 Marseille, France

Website: www.marseille.fr/culture/patrimoine-culturel/la-maison-diamantée

Useful tips: It's located near the Old Port, making it a convenient stop while exploring the area. Make sure to bring your camera; the distinctive façade makes for excellent photos.

LA VIEILLE CHARITÉ

La Vieille Charité is a beautifully restored 17th-century almshouse in the heart of the Le Panier district. It was originally built as a place of refuge for the city's poor and now serves as a cultural center housing museums, galleries, and a cinema. The complex is centered around a picturesque courtyard and chapel with a remarkable domed roof.

Location: 2 Rue de la Charité, 13002 Marseille, France

Website: https://vieille-charite-marseille.com/

Useful tips: Be sure to check the schedule for temporary exhibitions and film screenings. The courtyard is a peaceful spot, perfect for a restful break.

DAY TRIPS FROM MARSEILLE

CALANQUES NATIONAL PARK

Located just a 30-minute drive from Marseille, the Calanques National Park is a natural paradise, known for its limestone cliffs and crystal-clear turquoise waters. Ideal for hiking, boating, and swimming.

Location: Between Marseille and Cassis, France

Distance: 25 km (15.5 miles) from Marseille

Tip: Visit in the early morning or late afternoon in summer to avoid the crowds and the heat.

AIX-EN-PROVENCE

A city of art and culture, Aix-en-Provence is renowned for its natural springs, elegant architecture, and vibrant cultural scene. Stroll down the Cours Mirabeau and explore its rich history.

Location: Aix-en-Provence, Provence-Alpes-Côte d'Azur, France

Distance: 33 km (20 miles) from Marseille, 30-minute drive

Tip: Be sure to visit the Saint-Sauveur Cathedral, a blend of Romanesque, Gothic, and Baroque architecture.

CASSIS

A picturesque seaside town, Cassis is known for its dramatic cliffs, sheltered inlets, and vibrant waterfront. Explore the Calanques by boat and taste the local white wine.

Location: Cassis, Provence-Alpes-Côte d'Azur, France

Distance: 26 km (16 miles) from Marseille, 35-minute drive

Tip: Visit the Cap Canaille for stunning panoramic views of the Mediterranean.

ARLES

Step into a world of Roman history in Arles, with its well-preserved amphitheater, ancient ruins, and the legacy of Vincent van Gogh.

Location: Arles, Provence-Alpes-Côte d'Azur, France

Distance: 90 km (56 miles) from Marseille, 1-hour drive

Tip: Visit the Fondation Vincent van Gogh to explore the artist's deep connection to the city.

AVIGNON

Once the seat of Catholic popes, Avignon is a historic gem with the magnificent Palais des Papes and the iconic Pont Saint-Bénézet.

Location: Avignon, Provence-Alpes-Côte d'Azur, France

Distance: 100 km (62 miles) from Marseille, 1 hour 15-minute drive

Tip: Visit in July to catch the famous Avignon Theatre Festival.

DAY TRIPS FROM MARSEILLE

LES BAUX-DE-PROVENCE

Perched atop a rocky outcrop, this medieval village offers breathtaking views of the Provencal countryside and is home to the stunning art exhibit, Carrières de Lumières.

Location: Les Baux-de-Provence, Provence-Alpes-Côte d'Azur, France

Distance: 80 km (50 miles) from Marseille, 1-hour drive

Tip: Avoid the crowds by visiting in the early morning or late afternoon.

GORDES

One of France's most beautiful villages, Gordes is a stunning stone-built town offering panoramic views of the Luberon Valley.

Location: Gordes, Provence-Alpes-Côte d'Azur, France

Distance: 95 km (59 miles) from Marseille, 1 hour 20-minute drive

Tip: Explore the nearby Sénanque Abbey, famous for its lavender fields.

SAINTES-MARIES-DE-LA-MER

This charming seaside town in the Camargue is known for its beautiful beaches, rich history, and vibrant gypsy culture.

Location: Saintes-Maries-de-la-Mer, Provence-Alpes-Côte d'Azur, France

Distance: 115 km (71 miles) from Marseille, 1 hour 30-minute drive

Tip: Try to visit during a traditional gypsy pilgrimage, which is a vibrant and colorful event.

L'ISLE-SUR-LA-SORGUE

Often referred to as the "Venice of Provence" due to its canals, this town is famous for its antique shops and lively Sunday market.

Location: L'Isle-sur-la-Sorgue, Provence-Alpes-Côte d'Azur, France

Distance: 105 km (65 miles) from Marseille, 1 hour 15-minute drive

Tip: Arrive early to the Sunday market to get the best selection and avoid crowds.

HYÈRES

Known as the oldest resort on the French Riviera, Hyères has stunning beaches and a rich history, with medieval streets leading up to a Renaissance castle.

Location: Hyères, Provence-Alpes-Côte d'Azur, France

Distance: 85 km (53 miles) from Marseille, 1-hour drive

Tip: Take a boat trip to the nearby Porquerolles Island for pristine beaches

END NOTE

Marseille, the vibrant and historic city on the Mediterranean coast, offers a wealth of experiences for travelers. Its rich culture, mouth-watering culinary scene, and fascinating history will captivate any visitor, while its beautiful natural surroundings and nearby attractions make for fantastic day trips.
We hope this comprehensive guide helps you plan your trip to Marseille and enhances your experience while exploring this charming French city. Be sure to take advantage of the various museums, parks, and unique experiences that Marseille has to offer.
Bon voyage, and enjoy your time in this Mediterranean gem!

Unlock a world of unforgettable experiences with Tailored Travel Guides! As your go-to source for personalized and meticulously crafted travel guides, we ensure that every adventure is uniquely yours. Our team of dedicated travel experts and local insiders design each guide with your preferences, interests, and travel style in mind, providing you with the ultimate customized travel experience.
Embark on your next journey with confidence, knowing that Tailored Travel Guides has got you covered. To explore more exceptional destinations and discover a treasure trove of additional guides, visit www.tailoredtravelguides.com. or our collection available
on **Amazon** at this link: www.amazon.com/stores/Tailored-Travel-Guides/author/B0C4TV5TZX or
on **Google Play**, at this link: https://play.google.com/store/books/author?id=Tailored+Travel+Guides

Happy travels, and here's to a lifetime of remarkable memories!

Join our Tailored Travel Guides Network for more benefits by accessing this link: https://mailchi.mp/d151cba349e8/ttgnetwork
Or by scanning the QR code

Loved Your Journey With Our Guide? 🌟
Your feedback makes a world of difference! If our guide helped you explore or enjoy your destination, we would be thrilled if you could take a moment to leave us a 5-star review on our product page.🙏

Simply click the link or go to any of our product pages on your preferred retailer website and **share your recommendations.**
https://www.amazon.com/stores/Tailored-Travel-Guides/author/B0C4TV5TZX

Thank you for chosing Tailored Travel Guides!

Discover your journey!

CHECK OUT THE ITALY UNCOVERED SERIES

 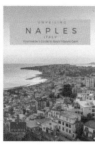   

ALSO IN THE SERIES

Printed in Great Britain
by Amazon

28805800R00025